THE TRIAL OF JESUS

The Trial of Jesus

Victim of Bigotry and Cowardice

Elio Palombi

Barrister-at-Law
Professor of Criminal Law
Department of Political Sciences,
Federico II University of Naples, Italy

Foreword by
Marcus Braybrooke

Retired Anglican Vicar
Former Director of the British Council of
Christians and Jews
Joint-President of the World Congress of Faiths
Lambeth Doctor of Divinity

BEACONSFIELD PUBLISHERS LTD
Beaconsfield, Bucks, UK

First published in English 2015

www.beaconsfield-publishers.co.uk
beacpub@gmail.com
+44 (0) 1494 672118

Italian edition © Pisanti Editori Sas 2009
English translation © John Churchill 2015
This edition © Beaconsfield Publishers Ltd 2015

British Library Cataloguing-in-Publication Data
A catalogue record for this book is available from the British Library.

ISBN 978-0-906584-68-2 (print edition)
ISBN 978-0-906584-69-9 (e-book edition)

Scripture quotations are taken from The New Revised Standard Version of the Bible, copyright © 1989 Division of Christian Education of the National Council of the Churches of Christ in the USA. Used by permission. All rights reserved.

Cover design by Ralph Hall
Cover picture, detail from 'Ecce Homo' by Antonio Ciseri. Image copyright, Galleria d'Arte Moderna, Florence, Italy. Used by permission.
Phototypeset in Times by Gem Graphics, Trenance, Newquay, Cornwall, UK
Printed and bound in the UK by Berforts Information Press, Eynsham, Oxford, UK

Foreword

Revd Dr Marcus Braybrooke, DD

Fifty years ago, the Roman Catholic Church made clear that neither the Jews of Jesus' time nor of later centuries were to be blamed for the death of Jesus. Thereby, they repudiated nearly two thousand years of anti-Jewish teaching by the Church which has contributed to the sufferings of the Jewish people through the centuries, culminating in the horrors of the Holocaust. In its decree *Nostra Aetate* (1965), the Vatican Council said, 'What happened in his (Jesus') passion cannot be blamed upon all the Jews then living, without distinction, nor upon the Jews of today… The Jews should not be presented as repudiated or cursed by God, as if such views followed from the holy scriptures.'

Other Churches have said the same. In 1988, the Archbishop of Canterbury, Robert Runcie, said at a Kristallnacht Memorial meeting, that 'For centuries Christians have held Jews collectively responsible for the death of Jesus. On Good Friday Jews have, in times past, cowered behind locked doors for fear of a Christian mob seeking "revenge" for deicide (the killing of God). Without the poisoning of Christian minds through the centuries, the Holocaust is unthinkable.'

Both in preparation for these statements and subsequently, Biblical scholars, both Jewish and Christian, have re-examined the Gospels' account of Jesus' Passion. There is general agreement that Jesus loved his fellow Jews and was loved by most of them. Crowds went to hear him preach, so that even the Pharisees said, 'Look the whole world has gone after him.' (John 12:19). Jesus had to be arrested secretly at night, lest there was a 'riot among the people.' (Matthew 26:5). As Jesus was taken to be crucified 'a large number of people followed him, including women who mourned and wailed for him.' (Luke 23:27).

There is much more disagreement about who was responsible for Jesus' death and about the accuracy of the Gospel account. There has been a tendency to shift the real blame onto the Roman governor, Pilate.

It is suggested that Christian apologists, at a time when Christians were being persecuted by the Roman authorities, wanted to show that Pilate had said that Jesus was innocent and that it was the Jewish authorities who plotted to kill him. Paul Winter in *On the Trial of Jesus* argued that the Sanhedrin (the Jewish Council) did not have the power to execute Jesus, so that it was the Romans who were determined to kill him. John Dominic Crossan in *Who Killed Jesus?* suggests that the Gospel accounts are 'prophecy historicised'. This implies that many of the events did not actually happen, but were added to show 'the fulfilment of what was said through the prophets' – thereby strengthening the claim 'it is written that the Son of Man must suffer much and be rejected.' (Mark 9:12).

In this important book Elio Palombi redresses the balance. As a practising barrister-at-law and Professor of Criminal Law in the Department of Political Sciences, Federico II University of Naples he explains the legal twists and turns accurately recorded by the evangelists, especially by John, and shows how Pilate was outwitted by the chief priests. The high priests, by rather questionable procedures and evidence, got the agreement of the Sanhedrin that Jesus was 'worthy of death'. Because the members of the Sanhedrin did not have the power to impose capital punishment, they could have let the matter rest at this point. Instead they were determined that Jesus should die, but to achieve this they had to convince the Roman governor, Pontius Pilate, that Jesus was guilty under Roman Law of lèse-majesté, a crime that covered cases of sedition and rebellion against the authority of Rome.

Elio Palombi explains clearly how Pilate, who did not regard Jesus as a threat to public order and who knew that he was popular with many of the Jewish people, was out-manoeuvred by the high priests. Pilate's gamble that the crowd would call for Jesus' release failed because the 'rent-a-mob' shouted for Barabbas instead. (John 18:40). In the end, the chief priests, who professed that 'We have no king but Caesar' (John 15:19), warned Pilate that if he let Jesus go, his job would be on the line. 'If you let this man go, you are no friend of Caesar. Anyone who claims to be a king opposes Caesar.' (John 19:12).

So, Jesus was put to death because of the bigotry and hypocrisy of the high priests and the cowardice and cynicism of the Roman governor.

As Ellis Rivkin has suggested, the real question is not *who* killed Jesus but *what* killed Jesus. 'The culprit ... is the Roman imperial system.' That imperial system is still evident in the economic and political forces which dominate our world today and allow millions to live and die in poverty and callously tolerates torture and the needless cruel and violent deaths of many people. To this we should add the equal danger of the perversion of religion to claim divine justification for the killing of innocent people.

Scholars, who may not agree with all of Elio Palombi's conclusions, will at least be challenged by this book to look again at the evidence and rethink their position. Clergy and members of the congregation will read or listen to the story of the Passion of Jesus with new attention and greater awareness of the importance of every detail of the Gospel accounts and their relevance to the world today

Marcus Braybrooke

Marcus Braybrooke received the Sir Sigmund Sternberg Award for Contributions to Christian-Jewish Understanding and in 2004 he was awarded a Lambeth Doctorate by the Archbishop of Canterbury in recognition of his contribution to international interfaith co-operation. His books include *Time to Meet: Towards a deeper relationship between Jews and Christians* and *Christian-Jewish Dialogue: the Next Steps.*

Acknowledgments

This book first appeared under the title 'Processo a Gesù' in a series published by the Department of Political Sciences of the University of Naples, Federico II. I am grateful to Professor Marco Musella, the Head of the Department, and to the Publishers Pisanti Editori for their kind permission for it to be published in English. I am indebted to the Revd Dr Marcus Braybrooke for enriching this edition with his Foreword and to Mr John Churchill for translating the text and taking it through to its publication here.

Elio Palombi

Contents

Preface

Who wanted Jesus to be sentenced to death? Was it the members of the Sanhedrin or was it the Roman governor Pontius Pilate? What role did the Sanhedrin play in the whole process? Some Jewish and Christian scholars – strongly influenced by a need to understand the reasons behind the antisemitism commonly ascribed to the Jews' collective guilt in condemning Jesus to death – have in general played down the significance of these questions, saying only that the crucifixion of Jesus was the work of the Romans and that all the rest is lost in mystery.

From that point of view the responsibility for the death of Jesus fell entirely upon the Romans for having taken up the case and then accusing him of lèse-majesté. However, such a version of the judicial process ends by clouding any impartial attempt to clarify the question of who was actually responsible.

If one considers that Pilate would not have hesitated to impose the death penalty on Jesus if his involvement in the grave crime of inciting rebellion against the occupying authority had been established, it is self-evident that he would also have acted with equal ferocity against Jesus' disciples, refusing to countenance the presence of an actively subversive organisation within his area of responsibility. It was obvious from Jesus' behaviour that there was no evidence at all of the sedition of which he had been accused. His teaching – a message of love and peace that was wholeheartedly shared by the common people – had nothing to do with the violent elements who were pushing the population towards rebellion and who were so greatly feared by the Roman governor.

Pilate was fully aware of the inconsistency of the charges raised against Jesus and the unbridgeable difference between the accusation and the actual facts. Faced with the choice of freeing an innocent person or condemning him to death, after terrible hesitation and for reasons of political opportunism, he presided over a flawed trial that ended with the rule of law yielding to the exigencies of politics.

Unable to resist the resolute determination of the Sanhedrin and to extract himself from a deeply embarrassing position, he decided to appeal to the populace and entrust to them the solution of this particularly unwelcome case. However, those who were called upon to make that decision in no way reflected the view of the general populace, being instead an excitable crowd spurred on by the Sanhedrin; and so the decision entrusted to a mob in front of the governor's palace was taken to represent the will of the whole of the Jewish people. The trial was in no sense properly conducted but was instead a spuriously democratic process in which democracy was used to bend truth and justice to the political requirements of the moment.

This book offers a reconstruction of the facts, as recorded in the Gospel story known to Christians through the centuries, from a legal and procedural point of view, reviewing the phases of the trial of Jesus as it took place first before the Grand Sanhedrin of Jerusalem and then before the Roman governor Pontius Pilate. Evidence from the New Testament and the early history of Christianity is combined with a scrutiny of all aspects of the judicial process, casting fresh light on the issue of who in fact should bear the responsibility for the death of Jesus.

Chapter 1

The Situation at the Time of Jesus' Teaching

In order to understand the charges raised against Jesus at the religious trial before the Grand Sanhedrin at Jerusalem, which preceded the political trial before Pontius Pilate, it is necessary to examine his life within the circumstances of the time during which he had been preaching, and especially so from 30 B.C. onwards. Jesus, who originated from Galilee, had arrived in Judea, a Roman province since 6 A.D., to spend the last days of his life in Jerusalem, to which great crowds of Jews had come for the celebration of Passover.

Everything appeared to be calm in Judea, *sub Tiberio quies*,[1] but in reality there was much underlying social tension. 'Public order would have been fragile because of the actions of zealots and other nationalists who were taking advantage of the reasons for public discontent.'[2] The Roman administration entrusted to the governor Pontius Pilate was an oppressive one that forced the population to pay tribute, and the heavy taxes that maintained the *pax romana* led inevitably to the impoverishment of ordinary people. There was therefore deep resentment towards the occupying force and a sense of resistance which at times exploded in widespread opposition, to such a degree that at the time of the annual pilgrimage to Jerusalem, as the tension grew stronger, Roman troops poured into the city to prevent any risk of disorder. Their heavy presence reminded the Jews yet again that they were a conquered people.

In addition to the oppressive power of the Roman governor there was also that of the local Jewish authority, a body intended to provide some nominal autonomy for their religious and cultural identity. In fact this body imposed further financial hardships on the populace, adding Jewish taxes destined for the Temple and the priests to the already burdensome Roman taxes. The livelihoods of farmers were in particular extremely precarious, since in addition to the exhausting nature of their work the combined taxation drained away what little they earned for their own subsistence. 'Farmers lived according to the rhythm of the seasons with

1

the aim of self-sufficiency in face of also having to cope with excessive taxation (from 30% to 70% of their harvest), harsh competition with other farmers for what little other good was available, and the unrelenting political restrictions on their freedom.'[3]

The Jewish population was controlled by a ruling class made up of the High Priest and the most senior priests, the elders and other dignitaries. These were supported by various groups such as the bureaucrats, the army, servants of the Temple and other functionaries employed in the service of the chiefs of the priests. The scribes and the Pharisees performed important duties concerning the correct interpretation and application of Mosaic Law. The Romans delegated some power which was exercised locally in Jerusalem by the Grand Sanhedrin, the supreme governing authority and tribunal of the Jewish community. 'The economic, political and religious life of the state revolved around the Temple – the source of every important initiative; a priestly hierarchy that the Jews regarded as ordained by God and which was fully respected by the Roman authorities. A structure in which religion, the administration of justice, the bureaucracy and, to a lesser extent, politics were all intertwined.'[4]

The Grand Sanhedrin of Jerusalem was comprised of up to seventy-one members drawn from the great priestly families, elders of the people, representatives of the local aristocracy and landowners, and lastly the scribes – the custodians of the tradition. A particular respect was maintained for the priests, who were for the most part Sadducees drawn from generally wealthy aristocratic families.

The Roman governor held the power of appointment of the High Priest, whose duties included the preservation of religious orthodoxy within the Jewish community as well as being charged with the delicate task of acting as mediator with the occupying authority. The High Priest was always fearful that his own local autonomy could at any time be overturned by a sharper and less respectful Roman response, as had happened after the riot during the governorship of Aulus Gabinius (57–54 B.C.), when life for the Jews became notably more difficult.[5]

The Jews therefore yearned to be free of their foreign masters and the heavy taxes they forced upon them. Even keener in all their minds was the desire to regain their self-respect and to be freed of the injustice and oppression that they suffered at the hands of their own Jewish rulers. 'Abusive and harassing, indifferent to the wretchedness of the poorer classes, imposing unreasonable further taxes and moreover spending them incompetently – such were the fragile circumstances in the Palestinian provinces, and not only in Judea.'[6]

In that climate of unending misery and resentment at the moral and material degradation of Jewish life, Jesus began to preach. He addressed his message of peace and love to each individual, speaking firmly against wealth and greed:

> *'But woe to you who are rich, for you have received your consolation. Woe to you who are full now, for you will be hungry. Woe to you who are laughing now, for you will mourn and weep. Woe to you when all speak well of you, for that is what their ancestors did to the false prophets.'* (Luke 6:24–5)

and:

> *'Again I tell you, it is easier for a camel to go through the eye of a needle than for someone who is rich to enter the kingdom of God.'* (Matthew 19:24; Mark 10:25)

When asked by a young landowner how he might reach the kingdom of God, he replied:

> *'Go, sell what you own, and give the money to the poor, and you will have treasure in heaven; then come, follow me.'* (Mark 10:17–21; Matthew 19:16–30)

His invitation was addressed to the conscience of every person, who, once liberated from the rigid interpretation of their religion would be spurred on to an awareness of their individual rights. The excessive ritualism prevented them from even realising to what extent they were exploited, removing any possibility that they could attain a sense of their own dignity. Mindful of that moral degradation, Jesus spoke scathingly of the servitude under which the Jews were compelled to live:

The scribes and the Pharisees sit on Moses' seat; therefore, do what-ever they teach you and follow it; but do not do as they do, for they do not practise what they teach. They tie up heavy burdens, hard to bear, and lay them on the shoulders of others; but they themselves are unwilling to lift a finger to move them. (Matthew 23:2–4)

and again:

'Let them alone; they are blind guides of the blind. And if one blind person guides another, both will fall into a pit.' (Matthew 15:14)

and ended by stressing:

'Woe to you, scribes and Pharisees, hypocrites! For you are like whitewashed tombs, which on the outside look beautiful, but inside they are full of the bones of the dead and of all kinds of filth. So you also on the outside look righteous to others, but inside you are full of hypocrisy and lawlessness.' (Matthew 23:27–28)

With its powerful appeal for equality and solidarity, Jesus' preaching was inevitably feared by the ruling Jews, challenging the status quo by pointing instead to the possibility of changing the world by acting upon the conscience of the individual: 'The world can be changed if first of all we are able to make deep changes within ourselves'.[7] His words were falling on fertile ground and making converts, and his miracles brought about ever-increasing successes among the crowds.

Jesus went throughout Galilee, teaching in their synagogues and proclaiming the good news of the kingdom and curing every disease and every sickness among the people. So his fame spread throughout all Syria, and they brought to him all the sick, those who were afflicted with various diseases and pains, demoniacs, epileptics, and para-lytics, and he cured them. And great crowds followed him from Galilee, the Decapolis, Jerusalem, Judea, and from beyond the Jordan. (Matthew 4:23–25)

The populace responded with enthusiasm to Jesus' message of faith and love and redemption whereas, alarmed by his words, the ruling Jewish classes were deeply concerned by it. 'Here already was the reason they should end by hating him so intensely and want to ensure his ruin; they realised their interests were at risk and were fearful of losing their position, with their doctrine challenged and their hypocrisy exposed.'[8]

The ruling classes were bound to move against anyone who threatened their limited Jewish autonomy as well as to act strenuously in defence of their own acquired privileges. It was especially true of the Sadducees, comprising as they did a true oligarchy centred around the grand families of the chief priests and the wealthy. This particular caste had full local powers following the abolition of the monarchy and the installation of the Roman protectorate, albeit under the strict control of the Roman authorities.

It is important to understand that some Jews had valid reasons for resenting Jesus. His teachings were in contrast to the religious orthodoxy of which the Pharisees were the guardians and who sought, by their strictness, to counteract the contamination of the country by the Roman occupiers. As the intellectual leaders the Pharisees and the scribes were the authority with regard to the practice of orthodox Judaism; the charges they brought against Jesus were therefore justified within that framework and arose from the contrast between their traditional rituals and his disrespect for such formal practices.

In 30 A.D. the Pharisees were the leading figures within orthodox Judaism in a society living under a widespread sense of malaise due to the two sets of taxes imposed upon them. If the real reason of the Sadducees was the fear of seeing their own power weakened, their strong opposition to Jesus was nevertheless justified by his attacks on their traditional rituals. The village Elders also acted as the protectors of the uneducated peasantry, who needed to be able to turn to an influential patron who would defend their interests; in exercising this protective behaviour the ruling class sought to numb their awareness of their condition, not least by encouraging these traditional rituals.

The Jews were bound to their religion and its formal aspects in an attempt 'to provide a kind of certainty for themselves ... its heavily ritual and formal nature, pushed to extremes, is symptomatic of a people accustomed to living under circumstances of great instability and therefore anxious to find some sense of security, whether real or illusory.'[9] In that atmosphere of exaggerated ritualism the revolutionary words of Jesus, exhorting the populace to faith and to the love of their fellow beings in the hope of imminent moral redemption, were unacceptable to many of the Pharisees, who saw them as a grave threat to the dogma and rules they imposed. Furthermore, the overwhelming popular support that accompanied the prophet's entrance into Jerusalem during the week of the Passover also perturbed the ruling Jewish class, against whose authority it was a direct challenge. Their resistance to the overwhelmingly attractive actions of Jesus therefore had deep roots, based on the need to protect their direct interests from being destabilised by his disruptive teachings.

'Added to the religious concerns of the Jewish authorities, evident from Jesus' first appearance in Galilee and which found their main expression in the criticism of him and his disciples by the Pharisees, there were also purely political considerations. These arose once Jesus had joined his disciples at Jerusalem and led to them approaching first the chief priests and then the Sanhedrin.'[10] Jesus was soon seen by the chief priests as a subversive element because his attitude towards the Temple began to undermine their power and affect their revenues, which the people in turn were increasingly refusing to pay. As a result there were important divisions within the Jewish community.

If the influence of the aristocratic Sanhedrin was primarily political it was the Pharisees who had the stronger hand, since their liturgical role made them the arbiters of true religious faith, charged with maintaining the effective functioning of the system and therefore strongly opposing the priestly high caste. And so the Pharisees were fighting a battle on two fronts: on the one hand they had to resist both the Sadducee oligarchy and the decline of Judaism caused by the Roman occupation, and on the other hand they were confronted by an unexpected and powerful competitor who was preaching a messianic expectation in strong contrast to orthodox Judaism itself.

The forces in play were therefore very unstable, at times involving them in a common purpose and at other times bringing them into conflict. There was the Roman governor who was charged with avoiding unrest among the populace, and there were the Jewish authorities who, in addition to their defence of religious dogma and the maintenance of public order, were also deeply involved in protecting their own privileges.

It was of course the chief priests who conducted the trial that would lead on to Jesus' death, but this objective would have been hard to achieve if the Pharisees and theologians were to have opposed the elimination of someone whom they too disliked because he was a threat to the rituals of orthodox religion.

Chapter 2

Contrasting Interpretations within the Gospel Narratives

Those who study the trial of Jesus from the Jewish point of view are often inclined to view the Gospel narratives as neither critical nor historical, and fail to acknowledge their value. It is accepted that Jesus was crucified on Golgotha but all else is subject to strongly contradictory interpretation. For example, who prosecuted him, who actually desired his death, and what role did the Jews play in the capital sentence imposed by the Roman governor? In other words, they assert that the accusations described in the Gospels are all driven by a desire to blame the Jews for the death of Jesus.[11] And yet, taken as a whole, the four Gospels deserve to be considered as a trustworthy representation of the events described in the oral tradition:

> ... *just as they were handed on to us by those who from the beginning were eyewitnesses and servants of the word.* (Luke 1:2)

and in John, too, there is a reference to the oral tradition:

> *He who saw this has testified so that you also may believe. His testimony is true, and he knows that he tells the truth.* (John 19:35)

Joseph of Arimathea and Nicodemus were indisputably eyewitnesses and in a position to report on the trial.[12] Nor should the fact that the Gospels are based directly on certain written reports be overlooked, as stated in Luke:

> *Many have undertaken to set down an orderly account of the events that have been fulfilled among us.* (Luke 1:1)

It does therefore seem unrealistic to believe that the four Gospels should have been a deliberate deception, written as they were at different periods and repeating to a great extent the same events, at times even verbatim. The earliest of them is Mark, written around 70 A.D., forty years after Jesus' death, followed by Luke in about 85 A.D., Matthew

8

in about 90 A.D. and John in about 110 A.D. In addition there is the Jewish testimony of Joseph Ben Matityahu (later Romanised as Titus Flavius Josephus) in Book XVIII of his *Antiquities of the Jews*, 93 A.D. In this work he described Jesus as 'a doer of wonderful works – a teacher of such men as receive the truth with pleasure. He drew over to him both many of the Jews, and many of the Gentiles. He was the Christ; and when Pilate, at the suggestion of the principal men amongst us, had condemned him to the cross, those that loved him at the first did not forsake him.'

In spite of this, the different dates of the four Gospels incline Jewish proponents to question their veracity. They maintain that in a period when Christians were relentlessly persecuted it was in the disciples' interest to portray the facts so as to exonerate the Roman governor and shift the entire responsibility for the death of Jesus on to the Jews. This explains the references in the Gospels to the fury of the Jewish elite against Jesus and Pilate's sympathetic attitude, shown many times, in his attempts to save him. Their desire to overturn the widely-held picture of the trial explains why they and those sympathetic to them emphasise the strikingly anti-Jewish tone of the New Testament. The whole story is queried, keeping Jesus' crucifixion at the hands of the Romans as the only certain fact in view of their exclusive right to administer that form of capital penalty. The texts are in all other respects assumed to be open to manipulation and at times to wildly fanciful interpretation.

This firm stance against Jesus, the grave charge of sedition raised against him in the political trial for having proclaimed himself 'King of the Jews' and Israel's Messiah, together with Pilate's repeated attempts to save him – are all dismissed in the search to put the entire responsibility on to the Romans. Why – if it was really the Jewish leaders who wished to have him dead – did they not proceed directly to execute him instead of consigning him to the Roman governor, with the unpredictable outcome of a trial in which they would have been the plaintiffs?

Furthermore, in the absence of any Jewish trial of Jesus it was for the Romans to prosecute a trial for lèse-majesté – an act of insubordination against Roman authority that led to a sentence of death. Jesus had been accused of sedition against Rome and the Jews had taken no part in the trial before Pilate. They often dispute the statement that there were two trials: the Jewish religious one before the Grand Sanhedrin and the political one before the Roman governor, asserting that if the Sanhedrin met together the night before the trial it was only an informal arrangement to make one last effort to save Jesus and persuade him to pull back from his already gravely compromised position, and thereby to prevent the execution of a Jew who was so deeply loved by the people. In other words, that it was necessary for the Jewish leaders to intervene in his favour once he had attracted the hostile attention of the Romans if a popular uprising was to be avoided, and by doing so to demonstrate that they had done everything in their power to avoid a tragedy.

Nor do the Gospels offer any reason why Pilate should have behaved in such a contradictory manner or shown such an interest in saving Jesus. Jewish (and some Christian) scholars are not convinced that Pilate would have found it difficult to take a grave decision in the case of Jesus. They ask how it could be possible to imagine that a cruel governor, well known for his hatred of the Jews, should have taken such care over a case in which he would have to pronounce a capital sentence for the crime of sedition. How could it be justified that a Roman governor exercising justice in the name of the emperor should have vacillated so long in the trial of Jesus? His authority was such that he could have him put to death without hesitation if he were convinced of his guilt – or else have released him at once if he found that there were inconsistencies in the charges brought against him. Either way, it is unlikely that Pilate would have found himself in an embarrassing position that could also have had serious consequences with regard to his standing with the emperor Tiberius.

In their refusal to accept that the Gospels were correct, some Jewish writers have maintained that the real enemies of Jesus were the Romans, whereas the Sadducees, scribes and Pharisees had no motive for wanting him dead. In their search for the responsibility for his death they also exclude any involvement by the Jews in framing the charges against him, putting these entirely onto the Romans. Why would the Jews have wanted his death? He was after all one of their own and they were aware of his many followers and how joyfully he had been received as he entered Jerusalem.

While not excluding the fact that the Sanhedrin assembly may well have concluded that the death penalty would be justified, the Jewish position is that it was their bitter realisation, and in no sense their true opinion, that having tried in every way to save Jesus they had no choice but to deliver him for trial under Pilate. Their urgent entreaties for him to withdraw his messianic claim had failed and it was therefore inevitable that the Roman governor would consign him to his death. 'He deserves to die' would then be the natural reaction to what Jesus had been saying, sealing him in the forthcoming trial to a fate from which there was no escape.

Seen in this context one must consider Jesus' reply to Pilate: 'You say that I am King', raising again his claim of regality even though it would appear to incriminate him in the charge of royalty brought against him. Pilate was still seeking to overcome his remaining uncertainties: according to Jewish commentators that reply was the confirmation he needed, since from this he could see that Jesus agreed. Jesus would therefore have admitted his guilt and the death sentence would then immediately have followed.

The Jewish reconstruction of the event can be confusing for those more used to the general Gospel view of who was responsible, and without question reflects a need to find the roots of the antisemitism commonly ascribed to their culpability in Jesus' death. The most difficult part of this, however, is how to interpret the role played by the Roman governor in the whole affair. His power was absolute, and it can therefore be argued that the ruling class was attempting to act on the Roman authority to spare the death penalty against Jesus. Supportive intervention by the Jews has thus been considered as clear proof of the defendant's rebellious conduct.

Were Pilate to have passed judgment on a crime committed by a subversive organisation active within his jurisdiction, it would have been very difficult to put Jesus alone to death while leaving his disciples free; in reality there was no evidence in his behaviour of the grave crime of sedition ascribed to him. His message of love and peace had nothing to do with the violence, so greatly feared by Pilate, that would incite the populace to revolt; and given that the province was already regarded as violent it is hard to imagine how the governor could have been prompted to impose a capital punishment upon someone whom the people had taken so closely to their hearts. This was all the more so, since he was deeply concerned to avoid any possible repercussion on his standing with the emperor Tiberius. There was no evidence that the accused was a dangerous rebel, nor any evidence of rebellion itself, and the charge of sedition was clearly unfounded.

Pressure had evidently been put on to Pilate by the Sadducees to whom, according to the Jews, a role completely at variance with the actual facts had been assigned. To speak of the Jewish leaders as acting as some kind of cushion between the ordinary Jewish people and a ruthless governor is to distort the reality of the situation. It takes no account of the deep resentment felt by the Sadducees against a preacher who sought to disturb the long-established status quo by attacking their privileged position and appealing to the conscience of the individual person. To say the least, it seems odd to maintain that the reasons for their resentment of Jesus are not evident from the Gospels. One can argue about certain passages but it is difficult to think that the Jews had no part at all in the decision to execute Jesus – or even that they had tried with all their force to save him from the bloodthirsty intentions of the Roman governor.

It is true that there are contrasts on certain points within the Gospels but what actually matters is the overall reconstruction of the narrative. Differences of times and places between the Gospel of John and those of Matthew, Mark and Luke are often highlighted to raise doubts about 'the case of Jesus' – and between these latter three writers the facts also sometimes diverge. Without attempting to assess the value of each of the different accounts it is more fruitful to draw from all of them, accepting that the various differences that certainly do exist will have arisen because the authors were drawing their material from many different sources. In any case, the additions that one finds in Luke and Matthew as opposed to Mark do not affect the actual framework of the trial. Nor is it the purpose of this book to examine any particular point that could make Mark more reliable than the other three. What interests us is the internal consistency of the facts combined with the reliability of the narrative of the complex events that led to the trial of Jesus.

Chapter 3

The Initial Charges, Collection of the Evidence, and the Arrest

It was inevitable that Jesus' teaching would be resisted by the ruling Jewish class. In addition to being a serious violation of religious ortho-doxy it was also an open and intolerable attack on their positions of power, and their decision to put a stop to his charismatic preaching dates back to the time of his first Passover in Jerusalem. It was then that he had expelled the money-changers in the Temple, throwing over their tables and scattering the coins on to the ground, as well as rounding on the merchants selling oxen, sheep and doves, telling them not to turn the house of the Father into a marketplace. It was in the outer concourse of the Temple that the daily social and cultural life connected with the sacred institution took place – the teaching, the sale of animals for sacrifice, and the exchange of the common currency into the silver Tyrian shekel. The presence of the money-changers was a consequence of the heavy requirement placed once a year upon the Jewish people that their payment of the Temple tax was only acceptable in silver coinage.

Jesus' forceful attack against the religious authorities and in particular against Annas – the previous High Priest, who was profiting from the flourishing trade on the edges of the Temple – was of course also a direct attack on their income. For that they seized the chance to castigate his actions, and seeing what he had done in striking at the merchants they asked him:

'What sign can you show us for doing this?' (John 2:18)

To which he replied with the prophecy about the Temple, alluding in reality to his own body:

'Destroy this temple, and in three days I will raise it up.' (John 2:19)

His response was used to raise a charge of sedition against the Jewish faith for having threatened that the Temple of Jerusalem would be destroyed. The accusation soon failed, in part because the witnesses' statements were contradictory but above all because it was wrong. Jesus had not threatened to destroy the Temple but in fact had promised to rebuild it in the event that others should have done so.

Despite the need to resolve their problem promptly in view of the imminent celebration of Passover, the leaders of the Jews were also clearly concerned about the possible reaction of the crowd if there were to be a violent attempt to kill Jesus. Already at the time when he attacked those who were profaning the Temple,

> *... the chief priests and the scribes kept looking for a way to kill him; for they were afraid of him, because the whole crowd was spellbound by his teaching.* (Mark 11:18)

In their investigations the Sanhedrin made frantic efforts to find evidence to support the charge:

> *When he went outside, the scribes and the Pharisees began to be very hostile towards him and to cross-examine him about many things, lying in wait for him, to catch him in something he might say.* (Luke 11:53–54)

Evidence was collected to question his orthodoxy with regard to his lack of respect towards their rituals and his violation of the strict precepts on the washing of hands prior to taking food. They challenged his healing on the Sabbath of a man with a crippled hand who then needed, in violation of the law, to carry his bed on the Sabbath. They also investigated his pronouncements about which punishment should be imposed upon the adulteress who had been repudiated by her husband. However, the material they gathered with such scrupulous care was inconsistent, to the extent that the chiefs of the priests and the elders of the people became alarmed at the way their enquiries were turning out:

> *Then the chief priests and the elders of the people gathered in the palace of the high priest, who was called Caiaphas, and they conspired to arrest Jesus by stealth and kill him. But they said, 'Not during the festival, or there may be a riot among the people.'* (Matthew 26:3–5)

They also challenged him about his conspicuous lack of respect for the Sabbath, referring to his sacrilegious statement:

But Jesus answered them, 'My Father is still working, and I also am working.' (John 5:17)

For this reason the Jews were seeking all the more to kill him, because he was not only breaking the Sabbath, but was also calling God his own Father, thereby making himself equal to God. (John 5:18)

Their decision to kill Jesus at all costs is evident from this obviously allegorical parable to which he enjoined them to listen:

There was a landowner who planted a vineyard, put a fence around it, dug a wine press in it, and built a watch-tower. Then he leased it to tenants and went to another country. When the harvest time had come, he sent his slaves to the tenants to collect his produce. But the tenants seized his slaves and beat one, killed another, and stoned another. Again he sent other slaves, more than the first; and they treated them in the same way. Finally he sent his son to them, saying, 'They will respect my son.' But when the tenants saw the son, they said to themselves, 'This is the heir; come, let us kill him and get his inheritance.' So they seized him, threw him out of the vineyard, and killed him. Now when the owner of the vineyard comes, what will he do to those tenants?' They said to him, 'He will put those wretches to a miserable death, and lease the vineyard to other tenants who will give him the produce at the harvest time.' Jesus said to them. 'Have you never read in the scriptures: "The stone that the builders rejected has become the cornerstone; this was the Lord's doing, and it is amazing in our eyes"? Therefore I tell you, the kingdom of God will be taken away from you and given to a people that produces the fruits of the kingdom. The one who falls on the stone will be broken to pieces; and it will crush anyone on whom it falls.' When the chief priests and the Pharisees heard his parables, they realised that he was speaking about them. They wanted to arrest him, but they feared the crowds, because they regarded him as a prophet. (Matthew 21:33–46)

The owner of the vineyard is God, the vines are the chosen people of Israel, the owner's representatives are the prophets, the son killed outside the walls of Jerusalem is Jesus, the workers who killed the vineyard owner's representatives are the Jews who have neglected their faith, and the rest, to whom the vineyard is to be entrusted, are the pagans.

The failure of their charges persuaded the Sanhedrin, in their determination to counteract Jesus' great popularity with the crowds, to change the emphasis to one of blasphemy for proclaiming himself to be the Son of God. Asserting that he was a false Messiah:

> *Then they tried to arrest him, but no one laid hands on him, because his hour had not yet come.* (John 7:30)

In that atmosphere of increasing hostility, realising that their charge of disrespect for religious ritual was not working, the Sanhedrin then changed it to one concerning Jesus' actual identity and his statement that he was the one and only son of God. Teaching in the Temple, he proclaimed:

> *'You know me, and you know where I am from. I have not come on my own. But the one who sent me is true, and you do not know him. I know him, because I am from him, and he sent me.'* (John 7:28–29)

They then began to have varying views among themselves about his identity and in particular the possibility that he might indeed be a prophet:

> *So there was a division in the crowd because of him. Some of them wanted to arrest him, but no one laid hands on him. Then the temple police went back to the chief priests and the Pharisees, who asked them, 'Why did you not arrest him?' The police answered, 'Never has anyone spoken like this!' Then the Pharisees replied, 'Surely you have not been deceived too, have you? Has any one of the authorities or of the Pharisees believed in him?'* (John 7:43–53)

A clear contrast began to be apparent between the resolute determination of the Sanhedrin and the wishes of the general public:

16

Yet no one would speak openly about him for fear of the Jews. (John 7:13)

It was obvious that the dispute with Jesus was with the ruling Jewish class and not at all with the masses, who continued to follow him with growing enthusiasm. The Sanhedrin, seeking in every way to find instances of clear proof against him, next turned their attention to his messianic claim. He replied:

'Can you say that the one whom the Father has sanctified and sent into the world is blaspheming because I said, "I am God's Son"? If I am not doing the works of my Father, then do not believe me. But if I do them, even though you do not believe me, believe the works, so that you may know and understand that the Father is in me and I am in the Father.' (John 10:36–38)

It was then that the Jews ...

... tried to arrest him again, but he escaped from their hands.

(John 10:39)

His adversaries further intensified their efforts to kill him, so in face of the impending danger:

After this Jesus went about in Galilee. He did not wish to go about in Judea because the Jews were looking for an opportunity to kill him. (John 7:1)

When it was the time of the Feast of Tabernacles he asked his disciples to be present at it:

But after his brothers had gone to the festival, then he also went, not publicly but as it were in secret. (John 7:10)

News of the resurrection of Lazarus at Bethany had spread rapidly throughout the whole of Judea, and the place where the miracle was actually performed had become the site of an enormous pilgrimage. The event captured the attention of the populace, and the anxieties of the

17

ruling classes increased further when some days before Passover Jesus decided to go to Jerusalem. The next day, on hearing that he was coming there, the great crowd that had come together for the celebration took palm branches and went to greet him, shouting:

> *'Hosanna! Blessed is the one who comes in the name of the Lord – the King of Israel!'* (John 12:12–13)

Such boldness could be tolerated no longer by the Sanhedrin, already deeply concerned by the growing success of a preacher whose vision of a society based upon human solidarity and social justice conflicted so directly with their own interests.

Moreover, in their view it was essential to eliminate Jesus because he was also a false Messiah with regard to the one the Jews were expecting – their belief that a great national liberator would come was even stronger since Rome had extended its dominion over Judea. The certainty of the arrival of a Messiah with regal powers was part of their yearning that the Kingdom of Israel and the Hebrew throne should be restored to their ancient splendour. But this preacher, who directed his attacks at the ruling Jewish class and who was so loved by the common people, could not be the true Messiah because in their collective imagination he would have revealed himself in quite a different way.

In every way the popular support in favour of Jesus' preaching was a real danger for the ruling Jewish class and their desire to deprive him of his personal freedom became even more urgent as time went by:

> *Now the festival of Unleavened Bread, which is called the Passover, was near. The chief priests and the scribes were looking for a way to put Jesus to death, for they were afraid of the people.* (Luke 22:1–2)

> *So the chief priests and the Pharisees called a meeting of the council, and said, 'What are we to do? This man is performing many signs. If we let him go on like this, everyone will believe in him, and the Romans will come and destroy both our holy place and our nation.'* (John 11:47–48)

which drew from the High Priest Caiaphas the solemn statement:

'You know nothing at all! You do not understand that it is better for you to have one man die for the people than to have the whole nation destroyed.' (John 11:49–50)

Jesus' preaching would in truth only have been a danger if Rome had interpreted his actions as fomenting rebellion and had therefore decided to intervene forcibly against the whole nation. But far from being an incitement to rebellion his call was an appeal to the conscience of mankind to bring about a great moral renewal. Regardless of the charges thrown at him, everything pointed to his innocence. 'He was irreproachable in attire, simple in manner and showed no ambition; he pointed the way to a law of love and solidarity that ruled the world; he loved the humble and poor; he identified with the distressed and rejected; he avoided pomp and power; he told those who held the power that his kingdom was not of this world; he paid his dues and was in every way an exemplary citizen. But he had often spoken out against the hypocrisy of the Pharisees, he had cried out loudly "Shame on the rich!", and had announced to the poor that they would soon be raised up.'[13]

His message of love and peace towards all, offered equally to the stranger as well as to the non-believer, had nothing to do with inciting the populace to revolt but was a serious danger to the ruling Jewish class, because in proclaiming the equality of all men he threw into question the whole basis of their power. The grave risk for the whole Jewish community that Caiaphas had hinted at was never in fact a real one since Jesus was not claiming an earthly kingship. Dante in his *Inferno* does not hesitate to place him among the hypocrites in the sixth ditch of the eighth circle of Hell, characterising him as the man who 'advised the Pharisees that it would be convenient for one man to be martyred for the whole of the people.'[14]

Reasons of state in the end prevailed, such that the High Priest …

… prophesied that Jesus was about to die for the nation, and not for the nation only, but to gather into one the dispersed children of God. (John 11:51–52)

and the Sanhedrin …

… from that day on they planned to put him to death. (John 11:53)

19

At this point:

> *… Jesus therefore no longer walked about openly among the Jews, but went from there to a town called Ephraim in the region near the wilderness; and he remained there with his disciples.* (John 11:54)

In the days before Passover a great number of pilgrims came to Jerusalem in search of him:

> *Now the chief priests and the Pharisees had given orders that anyone who knew where Jesus was should let them know, so that they might arrest him.* (John 11:57)

and it was here on the Thursday evening in the Garden of Gethsemane that Judas Iscariot betrayed him to the Temple guards, thereby causing him to be arrested:

> *Immediately, while he was still speaking, Judas, one of the twelve, arrived; and with him there was a crowd with swords and clubs, from the chief priests, the scribes, and the elders. Now the betrayer had given them a sign, saying, 'The one I will kiss is the man; arrest him and lead him away under guard.' So when he came, he went up to him at once and said, 'Rabbi!' and kissed him. Then they laid hands on him and arrested him. But one of those who stood near drew his sword and struck the slave of the high priest, cutting off his ear. Then Jesus said to them, 'Have you come out with swords and clubs to arrest me as though I were a bandit? Day after day I was with you in the temple teaching, and you did not arrest me. But let the scriptures be fulfilled.' All of them deserted him and fled. A certain young man was following him, wearing nothing but a linen cloth. They caught hold of him, but he left the linen cloth and ran off naked.*
> (Mark 14: 43–52)

According to John, but not to the other Gospels, Roman soldiers together with the Sanhedrin militia took part in the capture of Jesus. This would suggest, somewhat improbably, that the Roman governor had already been involved from the initial phase that led to the arrest:

So Judas brought a detachment of soldiers together with police from the chief priests and the Pharisees, and they came there with lanterns and torches and weapons. (John 18:3)

It is unlikely that troops from the Roman barracks in the Antonia Fortress would have been present at the time of his arrest. If Roman soldiers had actually been present there is little doubt that they, and not the Sanhedrin, would have taken Jesus into custody.

Chapter 4

The Trial before the Grand Sanhedrin of Jerusalem

Prior to the start of the trial before the Grand Sanhedrin the High Priest Caiaphas, well aware of the difficulties in the case presented to him for a preliminary examination of Jesus, decided to take advantage of the experience and authority of Annas, his predecessor and father-in-law. Annas, a person of uncommon diplomatic skill who had been High Priest from 6 A.D. to 15 A.D. under the rule of Augustus, still retained enormous prestige to the extent that for Caiaphas he represented a safe first point of reference.

The main purpose of Annas' interrogation with regard to securing useful elements for the forthcoming trial was to learn about the nature of Jesus' teaching. Jesus, in his dignified dismissal of the insinuations made against him and his disciples, answered:

'I have spoken openly to the world; I have always taught in synagogues and in the temple, where all the Jews come together. I have said nothing in secret. Why do you ask me? Ask those who heard what I said them; they know what I said.' (John 18:20–21)

This response was seen as distinctly insolent from a defendant who ought to have shown greater respect towards the High Priest during an interrogation. His behaviour was seen as sufficiently arrogant that:

When he had said this, one of the police standing nearby struck Jesus on the face, saying 'Is that how you answer the high priest?' (John 18:22)

To which Jesus replied:

'If I have spoken wrongly, testify to the wrong. But if I have spoken rightly, why do you strike me?' (John 18:23)

22

At that point Jesus was not just struck once but treated in a more painful and degrading way:

Then they spat in his face and struck him; and some slapped him, saying, 'Prophesy to us, you Messiah! Who is it that struck you?' (Matthew 26:67–68)

Now the men who were holding Jesus began to mock him and beat him; they also blindfolded him and kept asking him, 'Prophesy! Who is it that struck you?' They kept heaping many other insults on him. (Luke 22:63–65)

Annas was clearly offended by Jesus' attitude, however dignified, and therefore did not hesitate to return him to Caiaphas:

Then Annas sent him bound to Caiaphas the high priest. (John 18:24).

The interrogation by Annas did not contribute in any useful way to preparing the charge, so in the night of Thursday Jesus was taken for questioning to Caiaphas' house where the formal gathering of the Sanhedrin was taking place. They began with a careful examination of the witnesses about his striking those who were profaning the Temple, his view about rest on the Sabbath day, and his miracles. On each of these points every one of the witnesses agreed with the charges, whereas no-one stood to testify in his favour.

Now the chief priests and the whole council were looking for testimony against Jesus to put him to death; but they found none. For many gave false testimony against him, and their testimony did not agree. (Mark 14:55–56)

According to Mark and John, the threat about the destruction of the Temple that was attributed to Jesus came from certain witness statements:

We heard him say, 'I will destroy this temple that is made with hands, and in three days I will build another, not made with hands.' (Mark 14:58) whereas, in reality, alluding to the Temple as his own body, Jesus had said:

'Destroy this temple, and in three days I will raise it up.' (John 2:19)

The witnesses' statements were not consistent and so, with regard to the rule that the testimony of at least two witnesses must agree if a verdict of condemnation is to be reached, it was not possible to confirm the culpability of the defendant. Notwithstanding the disorganisation of their statements, the care with which these were considered – according to many commentators – demonstrates the correctness of the procedures that the judiciary were determined to follow. 'The due process of the law was carefully followed in the trial by the Grand Sanhedrin, which was not at all the farce that people have supposed.'[15] The charge was not taken as proved because it was not supported by the evidence obtained, thereby confirming the propriety of the Sanhedrin procedure. It was therefore 'a trial in full accordance with the necessary guarantees to seek out the issues of truth and responsibility.'[16]

This attention to procedure does appear to have protected the rights of the accused to be defended in accordance with Jewish Law, which demanded absolute rigour in taking the evidence of the charge. The influence of the Pharisees was notably strong in this respect, dealing primarily with the administrative and bureaucratic issues involved in the maintenance of an orderly society under the law.

This rigour was respected, despite the powerful influence of the wealthy and conservative aristocratic class of the Sadducees, who were determined to maintain both their dominant position and also the fragile equilibrium that existed between the occupying power and the defence of traditional Judaism. To that end the chiefs of the priests and the elders, themselves predominantly rich landowners, made use of the scribes against whom, among others, Jesus had directed his accusations. In their role as the functionaries of the Jewish community the scribes represented a united group that collaborated closely with the priests in managing the judicial proceedings and everyday activities of the Sanhedrin.

And so the religious trial of Jesus began, duly respectful of legal process and with particular caution in view of its possibly negative effect because of the defendant's wide following among the common people. If in fact the trial was broadly characterised by a respect for the accused person and did not exclude the presumption of innocence of the culprit, it would be even less possible in this particular case for the procedural rules to be disregarded. It was especially so because the Sanhedrin, mindful of the support Jesus had from the populace, wished to show that this prominent trial was conducted in a way that respected both religious ritual and legal formality.

Faced with the grave charge of violating orthodox religion that had made the appearance before the Sanhedrin inevitable, the scrupulous rules intended to protect the rights of the accused were not in fact strong enough to ensure the correctness of the trial. The doubts were centred above all on the impartiality of the judges. 'Reference alone to the law, the unique source of political legitimacy, defines the institutional role of the judiciary. This role – independent of the political system and unrelated to the particular interests of the protagonists – is based on the impartiality of the judiciary. It derives its legitimacy from the twin purposes of the law – the pursuit of truth and the protection of fundamental rights.'[17]

The trial was in fact only apparently correct in this regard. It was distorted by the determination of the Sanhedrin to influence the choices and act with vigour on the investigations, so as to move at any price to a guilty verdict that would then lead the Roman governor to inflict the death penalty. The Sanhedrin 'did not convene for any other reason than to declare Jesus punishable by death for his failure to observe a religious duty – a crime far more serious than the occasional lapse of some external formality.'[18]

The unrelenting tenacity of the Sanhedrin was clearly based on the widespread approval his preaching had gained among the populace, appealing as it did to the deepest part of the individual conscience:

Every day he was teaching in the temple. The chief priest, the scribes, and the leaders of the people kept looking for a way to kill him; but they did not find anything they could do, for all the people were spellbound by what they heard. (Luke 19:47–48)

The reasons for the Sanhedrin's antagonism towards Jesus were clear from the content of his preaching. He sought to change the minds of people and liberate them from the heavy yoke under which they had to live, and spoke with vehemence against the scribes and the Pharisees. And then there had been his violent striking of the merchants in the Temple, which the Pharisees regarded as a heretical attack upon Judaism – an exhortation to a moral renewal that would inevitably lead to the rupture of the prevailing orthodoxy.

Fervour such as this was a direct challenge to the authority of the Sanhedrin which they could not tolerate indefinitely. It would have been possible for them to complete the trial in short order, but the prominence of the case and their fear of the reaction of the crowd made them move more cautiously. 'The only thing that held them back was the mood of the public. It was necessary that Jesus should die to avoid a public uprising, but his death could equally lead to turbulence and the risk of public disorder.'[19] In the face of his mounting popular success the Sanhedrin could not but be alarmed.

On the other hand it could be argued that there would have been no personal reason related to protecting their privileges in their determination to exterminate Jesus. Their preoccupation was fully justified, being linked to the necessity of defending religious orthodoxy. Furthermore, 'it was the duty of the Sanhedrin to secure the death of Jesus to safeguard the religious integrity of their nation and not to undermine the working relationship they had developed with the occupying Roman force.'[20]

Protecting their Hebrew identity could also justify the Sanhedrin's charges against him, since in a deeply theocratic society it was essential for the control exercised by the ecclesiastical authorities to be both detailed and clearly defined. The rights of an individual were of no consequence in the system imposed on them by the powerful ecclesiastical organisation that was able to assure tranquillity in the name of the religious leaders – the whole of a Jewish person's life being based around the scrupulous observance of religious rituals that involved strict respect for the laws that governed their everyday activities. This also demanded an equal respect for religious ceremony that in turn would point all thoughts to a constant awareness of God. Ritualism so dominated the entire life of the people that it led to levels of fanaticism that left them completely unaware of the destitution in which they were obliged to live.

If therefore there had been a sound reason to charge Jesus for seeking to encourage a revolt against formal religion, it would not at the same time have been possible to justify the risks faced by the Jewish community with regard to a possible intervention by the occupying forces to suppress any subversive action. It is true that the Sanhedrin had the task of keeping the balance between the Roman occupiers and the Jewish local authorities; any hint of subversion would have damaged that relationship, with the risk of even heavier Roman domination and a far less respectful treatment of the fundamental values of the Jewish people. In truth, however, in view of the great following that Jesus had gained, the greatest danger did not arise from the claim that he was inciting the public to revolt; it was rather that if he were put to death there would be a violent reaction among a public ever more enthused by his teachings.

The actions of the Sanhedrin were of course not to do with the defence of public order but simply a pretext for safeguarding their own privileges. Their anxieties increased steadily as the public approval of Jesus also increased, to the point that they did not hesitate to launch attacks upon him, and his eventual sentence was in large part driven by their determination to stem the fame that he enjoyed. Challenged in its dogma, its interests threatened and subject to widespread invective, the ruling class could no longer tolerate the spread of revolutionary ideas, yet they were also aware that the death of Jesus could lead to uprisings with the consequent risk to public order.

His trial and condemnation therefore involved the serious danger of a public reaction by people who had heard his message of hope and redemption. Perfectly aware of this, the Sanhedrin took particular care in drawing up the case again him. Summary execution was not an option because of their fear of public reaction – they wanted to convince the public that the verdict was a just one that had been reached with scrupulous regard to the law. Despite their careful attention to procedural rules the trial was of course contrived with the sole purpose of securing Jesus' conviction. That is, the Sanhedrin sought to mask, by their strict adherence to the rules, their firm intention to eliminate him.

To clarify the motives which led to the trial being a parody of justice it is enough to reflect on the terrible treatment to which he was subjected. The cornerstone of justice is complete impartiality and in the normal process of law a third party, the judge, is present at the contest between the accuser and the accused – *processus est actus trium personarum, actoris, rei, judicis.* Due legal process is there to regulate the outcome so that truth and justice can be achieved within the framework laid down within the system of law.

In any event, the essence of the trial process is that the judge's role is one of complete impartiality. Therefore only when the verdict has been pronounced by an impartial judge can a trial be regarded as correctly concluded. 'Replacing an independent judge with an arbiter of one's own choosing is without question an established human response, not only in times of revolution: from the time of Jesus' trial onwards there has been ample testimony of judgments issued by the victors over the losers.'[21] The religious trial of Jesus held before the Sanhedrin was thus a pseudo-trial, a 'non-trial' because the judgment was entirely biased. It was a court of justice deprived of that fundamental impartiality which, beyond all the formalities, could have guaranteed that the trial would be both correct and just.

Chapter 5

The Interrogation of the Defendant

The one-sidedness of the Sanhedrin judgment is seen even more clearly in the intensity of the next stage of the trial, which then led to proclaiming that Jesus should be put to death. The vague and contradictory statements of the witnesses had obliged the judges to search elsewhere for incriminating evidence in the subsequent phase of his interrogation.

Jesus refused to recognise the charge or the trial itself and made no attempt to defend himself, responding instead to the attacks with a dignified silence. In reality 'he was condemned more for his utter silence than for the acts of which he was held to be guilty.'[22] This intransigent attitude and his significant silences were seen as contempt for the authority of the whole process, and in speaking solely to state the truth he infuriated those ranged against him. They on the other hand deemed it necessary to be unyielding when dealing with a completely uncooperative defendant who refused to recognise his culpability in face of the evidence.

It was that silence which allowed the Sanhedrin to act resolutely against someone who had turned away from the dogma, who stubbornly insisted on disregarding orthodox faith, and who indeed deserved no clemency whatsoever for having repudiated or – more precisely – actually scorned the rituals laid down by the priestly class.

Furthermore, the dignity of Jesus' silence prompted Caiaphas, leading on from the biased witness statements, to ask him:

'Have you no answer? What is it that they testify against you?' (Mark 14:60)

But he did not reply, and the High Priest then asked provocatively:

'Are you the Messiah, the Son of the Blessed One?' (Mark 14:61)

to which Jesus replied:

'I am; and "you will see the Son of Man seated at the right hand of the Power" and "coming with the clouds of heaven."' (Mark 14:62)

29

At that point Caiaphas, having got the evidence he had been looking for, tore his clothes and said:

> *'Why do we still need witnesses? You have heard his blasphemy! What is your decision?' All of them condemned him as deserving death.*
> (Mark 14:63–64)

The crime of blasphemy, committed in front of all those who were present, made it possible for the trial to move to a more secure footing. It queried the basis of Jesus' messianic claim even though it was anything but true blasphemy, because the Jews were waiting for a saviour who was a man and not in any sense a supernatural being.

In fact, Jesus' claim represented no offence against God, nor had the crime of blasphemy ever actually been raised before against anyone who said that he was a Messiah. And there was nothing about Jesus that had the character of the Messiah awaited by the Jews – with his humble behaviour and his miserable status as a prisoner he would never have been seen as a false messiah and accordingly been guilty of blasphemy.

It is correct that the duty of the Sanhedrin was to safeguard orthodox religion. But if they were to charge Jesus with blasphemy they would also have to show that there had been an attack against the Divine Majesty, whereas he was accused for his effrontery in proclaiming himself to be the Messiah and Son of God. However, the very basis of the charge was disintegrating in face of the observation that his claim to be the Messiah was in no way an offence against God, since he was simply referring to the identity of the person sent to Earth by God. By the same token, the statement that he was the 'Son of the Blessed One' was no kind of profanity against the name of God since it did not constitute a blasphemy against the Divine Majesty. This would only ever be the case where a person should curse God, pronouncing the name *Yahweh*.

Clearly, the procedure to ensure that Jesus was found guilty of a capital offence was heavily influenced by the Sanhedrin's determination to eliminate him. Their need to reach a guilty verdict, regardless of the fact that the evidence was flawed, obliged them – always respectful of the procedural rules – to violate the law themselves by assuming the right to use Jesus' own words as evidence of his blasphemy.

In a dramatic change of direction, stressing that Jesus had been caught red-handed, the High Priest's action in tearing his clothes gave symbolic expression to his conviction that the defendant was entirely guilty of blasphemy. Jesus' assertions with regard to his own position were manipulated in an astonishing crescendo to secure the required verdict while the earlier witness statements were rapidly abandoned. Therefore, regardless of the inconsistency of the charges, the Sanhedrin reached the decision that the defendant was guilty of a capital offence and should be put to death, solely to protect the interests of their own caste, and no obstacle at all would have prevented them from doing so. The absence of an impartial judiciary ended by compromising a fundamental principle of the trial.

Confident that they had found Jesus in the act of committing blasphemy, the Sanhedrin were concerned not to do anything that would reveal the invalidity of the procedure they had followed during the night. They therefore reconvened the assembly at sunrise the following morning, Friday to adopt their definitive decision.

When morning came, all the chief priests and the elders of the people conferred together against Jesus in order to bring about his death. They bound him, led him away, and handed him over to Pilate the governor. (Matthew 27:1–2)

The highest Jewish tribunal had therefore accepted the proof of the charge of blasphemy against Jesus and confirmed the death penalty upon him. Their decision was to have a profound impact on all those who had come to Jerusalem to celebrate Passover, but above all on a subsequent decision that would have to be taken by Pontius Pilate. The original charge of blasphemy was dropped and adroitly changed into the charge that Jesus, as a false messiah, had dared to proclaim himself King of the Jews, thereby threatening to undermine the social stability established by the foreign occupiers.

The charge of blasphemy was the means to the end as it was to be the basis for the charge within the political trial in front of the Roman governor, the only person who had the authority to inflict the death penalty for subversion. The definitive proof of the lack of impartiality of the Sanhedrin judges therefore lies in the manipulation of the charge of blasphemy. It became a political case in which Jesus had to defend himself before the Roman governor, who would then be able to pass the judgment so fervently desired by the Sanhedrin.

Chapter 6

The Sanhedrin Sentence

In their desire to eliminate Jesus the Sanhedrin had drawn particular attention to his insolence in proclaiming himself to be the Messiah. The trial before the Grand Sanhedrin furthermore went on to accuse him for blasphemously daring to proclaim that he was the Son of God. The Grand Sanhedrin had full authority to rule on cases that violated Judaic law, including blasphemy, which they held to be one of the gravest crimes against their faith and which was punishable by death by stoning.

Anyone who curses God shall bear the sin. One who blasphemes the name of the Lord shall be put to death; the whole congregation shall stone the blasphemer. Aliens as well as citizens, when they blaspheme the Name, shall be put to death. (Leviticus 24:15–16)

The Jews had tried on numerous occasions to have Jesus stoned for offences against their religion, which allowed for one God alone, and could not tolerate a declaration which for them amounted to blasphemy:

'Very truly, I tell you, before Abraham was, I am.' (John 8:58)

and so:

... they picked up stones to throw at him, but Jesus hid himself and went out of the temple. (John 8:59)

Later on, in the Portico of Solomon and early in the third year of his preaching, he was asked by the Jews to say whether he was indeed the Christ. He said:

'The Father and I are one.' (John 10:30)

This led to a further attempt on their part:

The Jews took up stones again to stone him. (John 10:31)

He responded, saying:

> *'I have shown you many good works from the Father. For which of these are you going to stone me?'* John 10:32

which drew the reply:

> *'It is not for a good work that we are going to stone you, but for blasphemy, because you, though only a human being, are making yourself God.'* (John 10:33)

Even though Jesus could at that point have been stoned, the Grand Sanhedrin decided in fact not to impose the penalty and the trial closed with a simple statement of the responsibility of the defendant.

All of them condemned him as deserving death. (Mark 14:64)
He deserves death. (Matthew 26:66)

The particular injustice of the religious case against Jesus rests in the fact that the messianic claim could not have been considered to be blasphemy and therefore that the Sanhedrin could not have declared the defendant to be worthy of death; in any event they were unable to enforce their verdict and so their sentence was not a real sentence. To declare that the accused was worthy of death did not also signify 'that he was actually condemned to be put to death, even if he was deemed worthy of that penalty. It was purely a solemn statement of responsibility, not a guilty verdict'[23], and as such would not have been subject to ratification by the Roman authorities.

A capital sentence pronounced by a Jewish court was subordinate to confirmation by the Roman governor and could therefore only be enforced after due scrutiny and ratification by him that it was legally sound. But the *exequatur* – the governor's authority for it to be carried out – presupposed that the capital sentence was legitimate under Jewish law and provided for that sanction, such that it could therefore be put into effect. Considering the specific charges raised by the Sanhedrin for the governor's required attention, it seems highly unlikely that, once he had verified the trial procedure and the appropriateness of the sentence, his task would have been limited to ratifying their sentence without a close examination of the merits of the case.[24]

According to this point of view the charges raised by the Sanhedrin would have been part of 'a refined trick intended to persuade Pilate into ratifying their verdict'.[25] In other words, the Sanhedrin would have surreptitiously drawn his attention to the dangerous possibility of public disorder with the sole purpose of securing his confirmation that their sentence could be carried out. If however a case of this kind were to have been treated as a straightforward ratification of the Sanhedrin sentence, Pilate, in whose presence Jesus now was, would not have needed to ask those who had brought him:

'What accusation do you bring against this man?' (John;18,29)

but would instead have limited himself to verifying the correctness of the trial procedure and the death sentence consequent upon it.

In reality the whole trial before Pilate became focused on the charge of sedition. The scrutiny he was required to make of the merits of the accusations advanced by the Sanhedrin went much deeper than being just a formal assessment of the legitimacy of the trial, and all his attempts to save Jesus went far beyond being a simple assessment of its procedural correctness. After studying the merits of the charges levelled against Jesus, Pilate stated several times that he had found no fault and that Jesus had done nothing to justify punishment.

Setting aside the fact that the governor's role in a case of this kind would normally have been limited to confirming the religious sentence, it has even been noted that since the Grand Sanhedrin were powerless to inflict the death penalty they should have limited themselves to declaring the defendant worthy of death, that is, guilty of a capital offence. Pilate had asked them to judge the issue according to their own laws: they replied that they were not permitted to carry out a death sentence, and that he was accordingly not restricted to ratifying the decision reached unanimously by the Sanhedrin but actually obliged to go further and condemn him to death by crucifixion. Under Roman law this covered lèse-majesté, which included instances of sedition and rebellion against the authority of Rome. If therefore the Sanhedrin were demanding that the governor impose the penalty of crucifixion one cannot also maintain that they were limiting themselves to asking him to ratify the death sentence pronounced at the religious trial.

Unable to impose the capital penalty but ardently desiring his death, the Sanhedrin 'were obliged to deliver him to the governor; but to do so they needed to specify charges that would be valid under Roman law. Within the wide scope of his discretion, the governor was able to consider such demands as the Sanhedrin proposed but was certainly not obliged to take the Jewish sentence into account.'[26] 'They needed therefore to convince the governor that Jesus was guilty of an act that was not only against their religion but also contrary to the maintenance of public order, and in doing so to achieve his execution.'[27] They had then to shift the emphasis to that of sedition against the authority of Rome.

'What then was the relevance of the religious trial of Jesus for an offence which was not a crime under Roman law? It would have been simpler to have brought the case straight to the governor.'[28] Nevertheless, although unable to carry out a death sentence they had exercised a basic right within the strictly limited context of their own jurisdiction – the Sanhedrin sentence was important in serving as a very serious warning to the population.

In view of the fact that the Grand Sanhedrin of Jerusalem had full jurisdiction in religious matters, this conclusion raises the question of what power they actually had in matters of penal jurisdiction. It is scarcely credible that their sentence for blasphemy against God, punishable by stoning to death under Judaic law, could not have been carried out by them in the event that the blasphemy did not interfere with public order as regulated under Roman law. (It would indeed have been possible, but they did not dare to do so because of the almost certain reaction of his followers.)

In seeking to obtain the death sentence the Sanhedrin found it necessary to imply that the religious crime of blasphemy would have implications for public disorder. Their unwavering determination is evident from the persistence with which they sought to break down the governor's resistance, even though he could find no evidence at all of rebellion by Jesus against the Roman authority.

Chapter 7

The Trial before the Roman Governor
Pontius Pilate

At first light on the Friday, with the religious trial concluded, Jesus was brought by the Elders of the Sanhedrin to Pilate to be immediately judged that morning. There was some urgency to finish the trial before the imminent festivals of Shabbat and Passover, so as to avoid the need for a resumption of the hearing at the end of the Passover festivities and the consequent detention of the prisoner. The Jewish leaders were fearful that the announcement of the arrest of Jesus could give rise to serious public disturbances among the great mass of pilgrims gathered in Jerusalem.

In the political trial before Pilate the purpose of the Sanhedrin was to support the charge that would legitimate their sentence upon Jesus in such a way as to justify a death sentence under Roman law. The trial was in fact stopped at the point when the guilt of the defendant had been confirmed, with no formal death sentence imposed. It appears that the Sanhedrin had declared Jesus 'worthy of death' for a grave religious crime, which under Jewish law would have been punishable by stoning to death, not to follow through with that verdict but 'to exert moral pressure on Pilate.'[29]

The Jewish tribunal was therefore not seeking a simple ratification by the Roman governor of their decision. They chose instead to submit the matter to him, changing the emphasis from the religious charge of blasphemy to one of sedition, punishable under Roman law by crucifixion and which he alone was able to impose. The messianic claim imputed to Jesus was therefore the pretext for transferring the trial to Pilate, who would then interrogate him on his royal claim, a violation actionable under Roman law. This basic ambivalence would soon become evident in the course of the political trial, which began in a state of grave embarrassment for the Sanhedrin in their meeting with Pilate, who asked them to explain the nature of their charges against Jesus:

'What accusation do you bring against this man?'

37

They answered:

> *'If this man were not a criminal, we would not have handed him over to you.'*

Pilate said to them:

> *'Take him yourselves and judge him according to your law.'*

The Jews replied:

> *'We are not permitted to put anyone to death.'* (John 18:29–31)

In reality the Sanhedrin, having charged him at the religious trial with the improbable accusation of blasphemy, were now trying to shift the responsibility of judgment on to Pilate, before whom Jesus would then have been obliged to defend his alleged royal claim. To that end they tried several times during the Sanhedrin trial to move the emphasis on to Jesus' subversive messianic activity, so as to establish in advance such elements of the accusation as would carry weight in the trial before Pilate. In this case the Sanhedrin, now changed from judges to accusers, had to prove to the occupying force that the crime in question had implications directly relevant to public order and that it thus represented an act of rebellion against the imperial authority.

It fell within the power of the governor to exercise judicial power over the inhabitants of the province entrusted to him. In particular, in the case of the *lex Julia de vi publica*, those who fomented riots and a revolt of the populace were to be dealt with rigorously and condemned to crucifixion. Moreover, in the interests of public security, the sentence would be carried out at once. On the other hand the governor had no authority in the case of religious crimes, which were tried by the Grand Sanhedrin under Judaic law. It is true that at times a violation of a religious character could also have an effect on public order, for example 'where preaching a doctrine against Judaism in a public space gave rise to agitation and rioting among the bystanders, who would then forcibly try to stop the insults to their religion. In such situations the Roman governor could not remain inert and had to punish the offender, either on his own initiative or under pressure from the Jewish authorities.'[30]

In the case of Jesus the Roman governor could certainly not remain indifferent to a problem which, according to the Sanhedrin, would have interfered with the power exerted by Rome. But according to Pilate the circumstances that would require action by him were absent, since the preaching of Jesus caused no disturbances or riots on the part of the crowd, who in fact listened to his teaching with much approval. It was the ruling class and the priests who were pressing the governor to intervene, sensing the danger that could arise from Jesus' message of moral redemption. Nevertheless, he needed to proceed with great caution because 'a decision by him that ran against the public will could set off the anger of the crowd and provoke disturbances many times more serious than those that they were seeking to quell.'[31]

The trial as held before the Roman governor was characterised by two strongly opposing considerations. On the one hand it was necessary for Pilate not to destroy his delicate relationship with the local Jewish authorities, and on the other hand there was his need to avoid disorders that could have seriously negative repercussions on his relationship with the emperor. He was well aware of these dangers and therefore did everything he could to avoid the sentence demanded by the Sanhedrin in their desire to demonstrate that Jesus had committed acts that would lead directly to public disorder. To that end they accused him of three things:

'We found this man perverting our nation, forbidding us to pay taxes to the emperor, and saying that he himself is the Messiah, a king.'
(Luke 23:2)

Jesus was thus being portrayed as a troublemaker by the Sanhedrin who were even hinting that he was guilty of *crimen maiestatis*, a crime that covered any and every act against the person of the emperor, even though at his trial by the Jewish authorities he had stated unambiguously that there was a clear-cut distinction between the earthly authority and the divine person. Perfectly conscious of their deceitfulness, they provocatively interrogated him on the lawfulness of the payment of tribute to Caesar, seeking to substantiate the accusation of sedition, to which he replied:

'Why are you putting me to the test? Bring me a denarius and let me see it.' And they brought one. Then he said to them, 'Whose head is this, and whose title?' They answered, 'The emperor's.' Jesus said to them, 'Give to the emperor the things that are the emperor's, and to God the things that are God's.' And they were utterly amazed at him. (Mark 12:15–17)

Full respect for the earthly authority, however, led to the collapse of the accusation that he had incited the populace to resist paying tribute to Caesar. Far graver instead was their accusation that he had said he was Christ the King. Claiming royal status in a Roman province, however, could be viewed as lèse-majesté since this collided directly with the authority exercised by the emperor. Pilate interrogated Jesus on that point:

'Are you the king of the Jews?' (Matthew 27:11, Mark15:2, Luke 23:3, John 18:33)

and Jesus answered:

'My kingdom is not from this world. If my kingdom were from this world, my followers would be fighting to keep me from being handed over to the Jews. But as it is, my kingdom is not from here.' (John 18:36)

Pilate asked him:

'So you are a king?'

Jesus answered:

'You say that I am a king.' (John 18:37)

Pressed by the accusations raised by the Elders and the priests, Pilate said to him:

'Do you not hear how many accusations they make against you?' But he gave him no answer, not even to a single charge, so that the governor was greatly amazed. (Matthew 27:13–14)

The claim by a person to be a king in a Roman province could definitely be considered an act of lèse-majesté, but Jesus remained silent in the face of Pilate's probing, having already expressed his opinion that any question of his reign in this world had simply no reality. His attitude excluded any possible danger of an attack against the emperor and so Pilate, who was trying in every possible way not to be involved in a dispute of a wholly religious nature, and who was increasingly convinced of Jesus' innocence, found himself in the dramatic position of having to absolve the defendant of any of the accusations, thereby bringing himself into direct conflict with the implacable wishes of the Sanhedrin. 'The man who had been brought by his enemies to Pilate to answer for criminal behaviour had shown that nothing about his behaviour could justify any verdict of guilty and that he was wholly beyond reproach or criticism. A parody of a trial had been prepared by the religious authorities who wished at any cost to strike down the one person they regarded as a rival.'[32]

To understand just how deliberate the manoeuvring of the Jewish authorities was it is enough to remember that they were using the charge of kingship to seek the death penalty, knowing that it had nothing to do with the subversive behaviour necessary to secure that sentence from the Roman governor. If Jesus had in fact been promoting riots, which by their nature would have involved other people, there is no doubt that his followers would also have been arrested at the time of his capture at Gethsemane, on the slopes of the Mount of Olives. It was not by chance on that occasion that he said, alluding to his disciples:

'If you are looking for me, let these men go.' (John 18:8)

And, in truth, none of his disciples were touched.

The claim of regality had no political implications as Jesus had made clear when he said to Pilate that his reign was not of this world. He had stressed yet again that if his alleged regality had an earthly content:

'My followers would be fighting to keep me from being handed over to the Jews. But as it is, my kingdom is not from here.' (John 18:36)

The accusation of regality that had been speciously linked to the messianic claim which triggered the religious trial would never have been sufficient to justify a death sentence from the Roman governor. Their demand for the sentence was based primarily on his preaching – intolerable to the leading Jews – because they felt it was his aim to strike at their positions of power. Subject to these external forces, and under pressure from the Sanhedrin, Pilate – ever more convinced of Jesus' innocence – was looking for any expedient to free him of the heavy task of having to take the decision they were demanding. Once again, turning to the Jews, he said:

'I find no case against him.' (John 18:38)

But they replied insistently:

'He stirs up the people by preaching throughout all Judea, from Galilee where he began even to this place.' When Pilate heard this, he asked whether the man was a Galilean. And when he learned that he was under Herod's jurisdiction, he sent him off to Herod, who was himself in Jerusalem at that time. (Luke 23:5–7)

The whole matter was therefore passed to the Tetrarch of Galilee, Herod Antipas, the son of Herod the Great who had reigned over Galilee and Perea. Jesus was immediately escorted by a group of guards into the presence of Herod at the Hasmonean palace, where he always resided during his stays in Jerusalem.

When Herod saw Jesus, he was very glad, for he had been wanting to see him for a long time, because he had heard about him and was hoping to see him perform some sign. He questioned him at some length, but Jesus gave him no answer. (Luke 23:8–9)

But his expectations were disappointed when Jesus maintained a dignified silence. Moreover, faced with the insistence of the chiefs of the priests and the scribes, who were reiterating their accusations, he decided to mock Jesus, joking about his royal claims:

Even Herod with his soldiers treated him with contempt and mocked him; then he put an elegant robe on him, and sent him back to Pilate. (Luke 23:11)

As a result, Pilate's embarrassment – determined as he was to avoid the death of Jesus – grew even greater. It was clear that Herod was also convinced of Jesus' innocence, because if not he would simply have stated that he did not have the necessary authority to examine the case; the fact that he sent it straight back was an eloquent sign that he too believed him to be innocent.

Pilate's difficulty is evident from these attempts to avoid making a definite judgment. The matter was weighing heavily and unfairly on his conscience and could amongst other problems also have had serious consequences for his own political standing. The Jewish court that was competent to judge Jesus had been the Grand Sanhedrin of Jerusalem and their verdict, over which Herod had no influence, had confirmed his responsibility for the grave crime of blasphemy. What authority could Herod have had over Jesus? 'He had none from a political point of view, since both of them were in a foreign territory and Pilate was not able to delegate to him any power in a criminal case. In fact, Pilate did not send Jesus to him for a judicial sentence but rather to get additional information and avail himself of the Tetrarch's opinion, if – as he supposed – he too would rapidly be convinced of the defendant's innocence.'[33]

Pilate then called together the priests, the leaders and the people and said to them.

> *'You brought me this man as one who was perverting the people; and here I have examined him in your presence and have not found this man guilty of any of your charges against him. Neither has Herod, for he sent him back to us. Indeed, he has done nothing to deserve death. I will therefore have him flogged and release him.'* (Luke 23:13–16)

He was clearly preoccupied by the need to free himself of this difficult case put to him by the Sanhedrin; they of course were equally resolved to take no account whatsoever of the consequences that would have followed the execution of someone so very much loved by the crowds. These consequences were clearly recognised by the Roman governor, who was seeking in every way to resist the insistent pressure of the Jews.

Chapter 8

Pilate's Appeal to the Crowd

The contrast between the Sanhedrin, who were pressing for the death penalty, and the Roman governor, who was seeking in every way to avoid it, becomes at this point dramatic. The Jewish leaders, who had no intention of pulling back from their position of complete intransigence, even hardened their position further.

In his desire to get out of this impasse, and with great crowds of ordinary Jews arriving in Jerusalem, Pilate resorted to the Roman custom of *privilegium paschale*, under which the decision on the fate of a political prisoner would be given over to the populace at the time of the Passover. This grant of power was appreciated by the common people and served to deflect their resentment against the foreign oppressor. The decision as to which of Jesus or Barabbas, both of them accused of sedition, was to be liberated could now be presented as a democratic one.

After speaking again to Jesus Pilate went out before the crowd:

'I find no case against him. But you have a custom that I release someone for you at the Passover. Do you want me to release for you the King of the Jews?' (John 18:38–39).

According to Matthew and Mark, Pilate spoke in more explicit terms:

'Whom do you want me to release for you, Jesus Barabbas or Jesus who is called the Messiah?' For he realised that it was out of jealousy that they had handed him over. (Matthew 27:17–18)

For he realised that it was out of jealousy that the chief priests had handed him over. (Mark 15:10)

The Roman governor was perfectly aware of the inconsistencies in the charges levelled against Jesus. He had to decide between freeing an innocent person, according to his conscience and beyond any motive of political opportunism, or handing down the death sentence that the Sanhedrin were demanding. He chose instead a third way – 'opening a

44

democratic process by appealing directly to the populace.'[34] In reality, 'the proposed choice between Jesus and Barabbas demonstrates how an authoritarian government can appear to heed the will of a governed people while actually concealing the need to put the burden of an unwelcome decision on to them and, at the same time, implicate them in that decision.'[35]

And so to get out of his predicament, knowing how the populace hated the Sanhedrin yet unable to resist their resolve, Pilate went to the people with reason to suspect that the assembled crowd was a mob manipulated by Jesus' opponents and in no sense a proper cross-section of the public. In addition to those Jews who normally came to Jerusalem for the Passover there were also others who specifically supported Barabbas's revolt against the foreign occupier and who had been encouraged to go to the governor's palace to demand his liberation.

Despite Pilate's awareness of the inevitable pressure on the crowd, many of them already influenced by external persuasion, it can be argued that he was behaving democratically in entrusting the choice to them. In practice this declaration of will was further manipulated by priests mingling amongst them:

> *But the chief priests stirred up the crowd to have him release Barabbas for them instead.* (Mark 15:11)

> *Now the chief priests and the elders persuaded the crowds to ask for Barabbas and to have Jesus killed.* (Matthew 27:20)

> *But they kept urgently demanding with loud shouts that he should be crucified; and their voices prevailed. So Pilate gave his verdict that their demand should be granted.* (Luke 23:23–24)

Pilate had thus been wrong-footed by the priests' incitement of the people, most of whom would have had no idea that they were participants in a power struggle. He was fully aware of the extent to which the populace hated the Sanhedrin and could not imagine that the same jubilant crowd which had greeted Jesus so enthusiastically the previous Sunday would suddenly turn against him and demand that he be put to death. And yet they chose to save Barabbas, even though he had been accused of murder during a riot and had been arrested by the Romans together with his accomplices.

Pilate's problem was clear: Barabbas was a rebel against Roman authority and a subversive individual, but he was also a public hero whose crucifixion could trigger a furious reaction among his oppressed fellow-citizens. But at the same time they were also deeply resentful of their harassment by the ruling Jewish class, so that once word of Jesus' death became known there could be the even more serious prospect of rioting among the mass of people who had welcomed him to Jerusalem.

Nevertheless, Pilate's wish to release Jesus was not fulfilled, because the crowd shouted in response:

'Not this man, but Barabbas!' (John 18:40)

He then said to them:

'Then what should I do with Jesus who is called the Messiah?'

All of them said:

'Let him be crucified!'

Then he asked:

'Why, what evil has he done?'

But they shouted all the more:

'Let him be crucified!' (Matthew 27:22–23)

It is obvious that the crowd in front of the governor's palace was expressing a heavily influenced choice. 'It was not a gathering of people in charge of their own ideas but a crowd whose collective opinion was being manipulated by others.'[36] The final decision taken in front of the governor's palace has since then been held to be valid for the entire Jewish people – a decision that cannot in any sense be regarded as a democratic use of power. 'This was not an example of democracy but rather the behaviour of an autocracy that flattered the public and then used them as pawns.'[37] Jesus by his preaching had offered 'in place of narrow rationalism a deeply personal religion, an adoration of God in spirit and in truth that threatened to strike the ruling Jewish caste by decreasing the amount of money they derived from the commerce that flourished in the Temple.'[38]

Pilate had known all the time that the Roman authority was not at any risk, that the crowd in front of his palace could have been silenced easily and that their views were not those of the populace at large. He saw through the flimsy evidence and found the charge of sedition unrealistic; he had no reason to believe that Jesus' claim to be the King of the Jews would be actionable as lèse-majesté, even though his behaviour might seem to have supported such a charge. Pilate chose to yield solely to placate those Jews for whom Jesus' attack on dogma, and above all his dangerous challenge to their privileges, had become intolerable.

Chapter 9

Pilate's Final Attempts to Save Jesus

The pressure from the Jewish leaders was unwavering and Pilate's sense of unease was increasing steadily. The idea of ordering the crucifixion of a man who gave no sign of being a dangerous rebel bent on subversion, as his accusers were maintaining, disturbed him profoundly. In an attempt to close the case without resorting to the ultimate sanction he decided that Jesus should be flogged to humiliate him before the crowd, hoping thereby to satisfy the demands of the Jews. A third time he said to them:

> *'Why, what evil has he done? I have found in him no ground for the sentence of death; I will therefore have him flogged and then release him.'* (Luke 23:22)

Pilate's hesitation led him to inflict a terrible punishment upon Jesus and the Roman soldiers carried it out with merciless ferocity. Not content with this they then began to mock him for his claim of regality; they cloaked him in a red mantle, placing a cane in his hand and a crown of thorns upon his head to dress him as if he were some subjugated king. They then presented him to the crowd, wearing the crown of thorns.

> *Then Pilate took Jesus and had him flogged. And the soldiers wove a crown of thorns and put it on his head, and they dressed him in a purple robe. They kept coming up to him, saying 'Hail, King of the Jews!' and striking him on the face.* (John 19:1–3)

Pilate's intention had been to avoid pronouncing the death sentence by ordering this solemn, public and humiliating punishment. He trusted it would be sufficient to pacify the tenacity of the Jewish leaders, showing that the man who proclaimed himself to be a king was nothing more than an inoffensive and miserable object of derision. Coming out of his palace he said to the Jews:

'Look, I am bringing him out to let you know that I find no case against him.' So Jesus came out, wearing the crown of thorns and the purple robe. Pilate said to them, 'Here is the man!' (John19:4–5)

But his plan was without effect. The chief priests and the guards were entirely indifferent to the sight of Jesus reduced to his pitiful condition and did not hesitate to shout even more loudly:

'Crucify him!'

At that point it was clear to Pilate that he had not succeeded. In his exasperation he replied:

'Take him yourselves and crucify him; I find no case against him.' (John 19:6)

Always anxious to avoid dangerous confrontations with the public that could arouse the displeasure of the emperor, he also knew how deeply the preaching of Jesus had affected the common people, realising that their reaction to the death sentence upon someone who wished so fervently for the redemption of the humble and meek would be un-predictable. But these political preoccupations came up against the determination of the Jewish elite who – having seen that the charge of sedition was not taken seriously by the Romans – did not now hesitate to revert to the religious charge on which the Sanhedrin trial had been based.

The Jews answered him, 'We have a law, and according to that law he ought to die because he has claimed to be the son of God.' (John 19:7)

In this way they sought to strengthen their case against Jesus, reminding Pilate that their response was in any event a matter of respect for the law and not one of personal hostility. Their tone was refractory, and Pilate saw that he had no alternative in view of the need to maintain the stability of his relations with the local authorities. Alarmed at the way events were moving, he now decided to interrogate Jesus once again, concentrating on his claims of regality and that he was the Son of God.

These could have had implications with regard to the emperor's authority, which at the time was increasingly being presented as being divine. Taking him back into the interior of his palace, Pilate asked:

> *'Where are you from?' But Jesus gave him no answer. Pilate therefore said to him, 'Do you refuse to speak to me? Do you not realise that I have power to release you, and power to crucify you?'* (John 19:9–10)

Jesus, whose behaviour was normally that of dignified silence, could not hold back from questioning Pilate about the governor's right to be in judgment over his life.

> *'You would have no power over me unless it had been given you from above; therefore the one who handed me over to you is guilty of a greater sin.'* (John 19:11)

Even though this seemed to imply that there was a link between divine power and earthly power, 'it is not a reflection on the divine origin of political power, as used to be thought; it was God's plan of salvation within which Pilate acts in condemning Jesus.'[39]

Pilate terminated the interrogation at that point, determined to release Jesus, being more and more convinced that he was innocent of what in any case was a non-existent offence. The Jews sensed his extreme embarrassment as well as his intention to release Jesus; changing their argument they pressed him:

> *'If you release this man, you are no friend of the emperor. Everyone who claims to be a king sets himself against the emperor.'* (John 19:12)

Taking advantage of Pilate's hesitation they now moved on to the attack, threatening to report to the emperor Tiberius an instance of his obvious disloyalty in having released a man who had proclaimed himself to be the king of the Jews. 'They, who loathed Rome, were now acting as though they were its staunchest supporters. According to them, they were bound to remind Pilate that being the king of the Jews and rebelling against Rome were one and the same thing.'[40] Pilate, a paragon of correctness, knew that the assertion was groundless but was unable to free himself from their hammering insistence, becoming more and more alarmed at the increasingly political overtones of the religious dispute.

Anxiety about his own position vis-à-vis the emperor had now become more important to him than the law and all trace of his indecision vanished. It was the day before Passover and he had Jesus taken outside of his palace at about the sixth hour. Sitting on the judge's bench at a place called The Stone Pavement, or in Hebrew Gabbatha, he behaved as if he recognised Jesus' claim to regality, pointing him out to the Jews:

'Here is your King!'

But the crowd became even wilder and shouted:

'Away with him! Away with him! Crucify him!'

Pilate wanted to make it entirely clear that he was passing the sentence at the insistence of the Jews. With scarcely veiled irony he asked them:

'Shall I crucify your King?' (John 19:14-15)

The Sanhedrin now knew that they had won and that their demand would be granted. To overcome Pilate's insistent question – asking them one more time to reflect on the gravity of the fact that he should be ordering the death of their king – the chief priests adroitly overturned the accusation, replying:

'We have no king but the emperor.' (John 19:15)

The Sanhedrin had hit the mark. Pilate, however, had succeeded in obtaining the chief priests' unreserved declaration of submission to the Roman authority. He delivered his judgment at once, implicitly expressed by his handing Jesus over to the executioners.

Then he handed him over to be crucified. (John 19:16)

On the Friday evening, before dusk fell, Jesus was crucified.

So they took Jesus; and carrying the cross by himself, he went out to what is called the Place of the Skull, which in Hebrew is called Golgotha. There they crucified him, and with him two others, one on either side, with Jesus between them. Pilate also had an inscription written and put on the cross. It read, 'Jesus of Nazareth, the King of the Jews.' (John 19:17-19)

The chief priests then said to Pilate:

'Do not write "The King of the Jews", but "This man said, I am King of the Jews".' (John 19:21)

The transcendent regality that had so radiated from Jesus caused Pilate to respond harshly:

'What I have written I have written.' (John 19:22)

Fully aware of the injustice of the execution, and perhaps also in an attempt to appease his lacerated conscience, he washed his hands. By that action he sought to justify to the outside world – and above all to the emperor – a decision that would have so many repercussions upon the population, upon the emperor, and indeed upon himself.

Chapter 10

Pilate: a Judge above the Parties, but an Opportunistic One

A true dialectic process finally began to emerge in the trial before the Roman governor. That is to say, between the Sanhedrin, who had already shown themselves at the religious trial to be wholly biased judges and who continued to maintain their position vehemently, and Jesus, who was submitting to the procedure with great dignity. Above the two parties there was Pilate; although capable of acting as an impartial judge he did not have the resolve to guarantee that judicial independence should prevail and so ended by giving in to the Sanhedrin.

It is necessary to examine the reasons that led him to yield to such outside influence and end by handing down a judgment born of political calculation. Jesus was put to death even though Pilate recognised that the person who was accused of being the king of the Jews was innocent, since there was no evidence to support the charge against him of subversive activity. Even though the evidence of sedition did not exist (and if it had existed it should have been analysed in detail), the trial continued. There was no crime that had led to a charge, but there was a charge for which a crime was being sought in every possible way.

How was it that Pilate chose not to save Jesus and end the trial with his iniquitous verdict, having found no evidence of the indictment by the Jews? He certainly had the widest possible judicial discretion in the matter within the inquisitorial system known as *cognitio extra ordinem*; this was the normal process in Roman law that allowed for an appeal to be overridden by a judge acting alone and with absolute power. Once a death sentence had been pronounced it was to be carried out at once (unless the accused did not have Roman citizenship, in which case there was the possibility of an appeal direct to the emperor).

He could have resolved the matter easily by acquitting Jesus according to his conscience, as any other judge with such full powers over the two parties would have been able to do. The absence of any proof of sedition, which would have been material under Roman law and formed the basis of a judgment, made the case particularly simple. Instead, although he clearly believed that Jesus was innocent, Pilate ended by making his own life more complicated.

What were the reasons for his vacillation? Why did he hold back from making a firm judgment in a case that was in no way unique during a period when instances of lèse-majesté relating to subversion had been increasing considerably? It would have been easy for him, the cynical representative of a tyrannical power, to view the issue on a par with other similar ones and settle it without hesitation. Philo of Alexandria described Pilate as 'intransigent, obstinate and hard' – a person whose methods included 'fraud, violence, robbery and torture', with ample evidence 'of extrajudicial executions and constant cruelty'.[41]

In sharp contrast to his reputed harshness, Pilate's behaviour in this case reveals him to have been lacking in courage and incapable of taking a firm stance. In particular, 'the pages of John's Gospel do not portray a man who speeds Jesus to his death with indifference, but rather one who attained a puzzling and undeniable humanity in front of the mystery of the man who stood before him.'[42] It is doubt that characterises him, and it is doubt that provides the human quality that redeems him. When he gives in to a fanatical multitude he seems to be a judge 'who violates the law because he is lacking in courage, skill, prudence and strength of character'.[43] 'With his hesitation and indecisiveness, and with his circuitous way of trying to foil the plans of the priests, he reminds us of a small provincial Machiavelli.'[44] 'His handling of the case shows him to be a political mediocrity. And even when he takes the initiative by entrusting Jesus' fate to the public it can be claimed that there would have been a delegation of responsibility, since he would not have had the moral capacity to make the choice himself. In this regard we can say that it was Pilate's moral weakness in the face of the determination of the priests.'[45]

However, to attribute Pilate's vacillation to a lack of courage – in a person whose position required him to take grave decisions in an extremely complex case – fails to recognise the true reasons behind the drama.

He was well aware that a decision to free Jesus would have created serious problems with the local authorities but above all with the emperor Tiberius, the man who had given him charge over a difficult province in which there was the ever-present danger of revolt. It is necessary to consider the reasons that made him unable to resist the pressure of the Sanhedrin, where a failure to satisfy their demands would have had serious consequences. Relations between the Roman and the local Jewish authorities were always difficult but Pilate, regardless of the contempt he felt towards their representatives, could not dismiss out of hand their request in a matter of vital importance to them.

Even setting aside the fact that the charge of blasphemy had been shown to be inconsistent according to the law, the strenuous objections raised against Jesus were disquieting because his claim to regality could have had implications with regard to the secular authorities. In fact 'with his claim of regality and his repeated allusions to the messianic predictions of a moral and religious renewal of the people of Israel, he certainly did provide grounds for this charge'.[46] Moreover, the single and completely specious charge of sedition could have created problems for Pilate, responsible as he was to Tiberius for public order under the fragile equilibrium between his occupying forces and the local authority. Any threat of sedition was bound to demand his close attention.

The problem was at its highest when crowds of people were flooding into Jerusalem for the Passover, so much so that during this period he would move from his normal residence at Caesarea to Jerusalem, where he lodged in the Antonia Fortress overlooking the Temple. His overriding concern was therefore to eliminate the possibility of public rioting. As a skilful politician he knew that his authority was in no way at risk from Jesus' claim of regality, but he also realised that he was in serious difficulty and that the politics of the situation would sooner or later involve him personally. He knew that the Jewish leaders saw Jesus' preaching as an unacceptable attack on their entrenched privileges, but equally that his death could have provoked widespread public disturbances among his large following. Pilate was not a weak person and his hesitation was based on pure calculation. 'His complex personality combines many different traits. He is brutal and violent, though astute and calculating; he is careful not to violate the Roman precepts of equity and justice, but even more so not to prejudice his own career.'[47]

Notwithstanding his unquestioned political shrewdness, the great difficulty he was now in led him to take a false step – handing over to the crowd his judicial role, and thus also the verdict. That decision, a product of equivocation and compromise, was an error from the outset and he should never have made it. It is hard to imagine that Pilate would have decided easily to entrust the judgment to the people, knowing that the outcome would be uncertain and that he would therefore be taking a grave risk. On the one hand there was a man accused of subversive activity but where no evidence had been forthcoming. On the other hand was a revolutionary accused of murder, an enemy of Rome and its imperial power.

The reasoning that persuaded Pilate was the emperor's possible reaction to any wrong move on his part. With regard to this case it is out of the question that he should have done other than crucify Barabbas, a known criminal whose activities fell within the scope of obligatory execution, especially in a province where the risk of subversion was high. The execution of a terrorist involved in serious crime would never have had the slightest repercussions for him since it would have been in full accordance with the requirements of the emperor. Putting Jesus to death, however, a person adored by the crowds as much as hated by the ruling class of the Jews, could have triggered a violent reaction. How could he have justified this to the emperor? In any similar case it would have been extremely difficult for him to defend such a decision.

The fact that Pilate decided to entrust himself to the public will was an instance of purely opportunistic politics. 'In contrast to the usual picture of a weak, scheming and self-serving man we can see in him a pure politician whose sole objectives were power and control and for whom all other considerations, truth and justice included, were simply the means to an end.'[48] Seen in this light he did not yield to the crowd as is commonly supposed but actually chose to do so, demonstrating to them that he was capable of accommodating himself to the expectations of the noisy crowd that was crying out for Jesus' death. 'The legal aspects of the case were overwhelmed by those of political interest. And in a political trial the fate of the accused person and even the sacrifice of his life count infinitely less than "reasons of state", in other words, the opportunism born of power.'[49]

Pilate lacked the courage to sacrifice any of his power and thereby to allow truth and justice to prevail. He swung between the two opposing choices but in the end consigned Jesus to the Cross, unable to resist the insistence of the Sanhedrin, whose motivation of course lay far beyond the original religious charge of blasphemy. At first he 'resists the pressure of the Sanhedrin, trying to free Jesus rather than Barabbas; later, as the opportunist he was, yielding to political expedience to deliver Jesus to the executioners. The life of a fanatical Jewish dreamer could not be worth his own prefectorial office.'[50]

Simply put, his primary objective was to protect his relationship with the Jewish ruling class so as to avoid the risk of any negative repercussions on the governance of the province. Pilate was thus the political opportunist, ready to sacrifice truth and justice to the overriding demands of government control – a classic example of the politicisation of the role of the judge, a function which should perforce be exercised in complete freedom from all external influences and in every case remain neutral.

References

1. Tacitus, *Historiae*, 9, 2
2. Zagrebelsky, G., *Il 'Crucifige' e la democrazia*, 1995, p. 37
3. Saldarini, A.J., *Farisei, scribi e sadducei nella società palestinese*, 2003, p. 58
4. Cecchini, G.L., *Pilato giusto giudice?* in Bonvecchio-Coccopalmerio, *Ponzio Pilato o del giusto giudice*, 1998, p. 267
5. Mommsen, T., *Storia di Roma*, vol. 4, I, III, no. 28
6. Pajardi, P., *Il processo di Gesù*, 1994, p. 113
7. Cecchini, G.L., *op. cit.*, p. 270
8. Di Miscio, G., *Il processo di Cristo*, 1991, p. 43
9. Pajardi, P., *op. cit.*, p. 25
10. Jossa, G., *Il processo di Gesù*, 2002, p. 33
11. Chon, C., *Processo e morte di Gesù. Un punto di vista ebraico*, 2000, p. 3
12. Blinzler, J., *Il processo di Gesù*, 1996, p. 146
13. Rosadi, G., *Il processo di Gesù*, 1919, p. 2
14. Dante, A., *Inferno*, canto XXIII, II, 116-117
15. Fabbrini, B., *Le accuse e le prove*, in Amarelli-Lucrezi, *Il processo contro Gesù*, 1999, p. 154
16. Pajardi, P., *op. cit.* p. 54
17. Ferrajoli, L., *Diritto e ragione. Teoria del garantismo penale*, 1990, p. 593
18. Blinzler, J., *op. cit.*, p. 176
19. Zagrebelsky, G., *op. cit.*, p. 41
20. Imbert, J., *Il processo di Gesù*, 1984, p. 163
21. Satta, S., *Il mistero del processo*, 1994. p. 34
22. Zagrebelsky, G., *op. cit.*, p. 23
23. Santalucia, B., *La giurisdizione del prefetto di Giudea*, in Amarelli-Lucrezi, *Il processo contro Gesù*, *op. cit.*, p. 103
24. Pajardi, P., *op. cit.*, p. 26
25. Pajardi, P., *op. cit.*, p. 14
26. Fabbrini, B., *Le accuse e le prove*, in Amarelli-Lucrezi, *Il processo contro Gesù*, *op. cit.*, p. 164
27. Santalucia, B., *La giuridizione del prefetto di Giudea*, in Amarelli-Lucrezi, *Il processo contro Gesù*, *op. cit.*, p. 100
28. Fabbrini, B., *op. cit.*, p. 165

29. Blinzler, J., *op. cit.*, p. 219
30. Santalucia, B., *op. cit.*, p. 98
31. Santalucia, B., *op. cit.*, p. 99
32. Galot, J., *La civiltà cattolica*, 1984, III, p. 123
33. Prat, F., *Gesù Cristo. La sua vita, la sua dottrina, l'opera sua*, 1954, II, p. 368
34. Miglietta, M., *Pilatus dimisit illis Barabbam*, in Bonvecchio-Coccopalmerio, *Ponzio Pilato o del giusto giudice*, *op. cit.*, p. 173
35. Miglietta, M., *op. cit.*, p. 172
36. Zagrebelsky, G., *op. cit.*, p. 93
37. Zagrebelsky, G., *op. cit.*, p. 100
38. Dessy, A., *Gesù davanti al sinedrio e al giudice romano,* in *Sindon*, 32, 1983
39. Ravasi, G., *Gesù davanti a Ponzio Pilato*, in Bonvecchio-Coccopalmerio, *Ponzio Pilato o del giusto giudice*, *op. cit.*, p. 5
40. Alfieri, L., *Pilato e la Verità*, in Bonvecchio-Coccopalmerio, *Ponzio Pilato o del giusto giudice*, *op. cit.*, p. 5
41. *Legatio ad Caium*, p. 301
42. Gatti, R., *Che cos'è la verità?*, in Bonvecchio-Coccopalmerio, *Ponzio Pilato o del giusto giudice*, *op. cit.*, p. 87
43. Blinzler, J., *op. cit.*, p. 283
44. Gatti, R., *op. cit.*, p. 82
45. Gatti, R., *op. cit.*, p. 77
46. Zagrebelsky, G., *op. cit.*, p. 56
47. Imbert, J., *op. cit.*, p. 90
48. Zagrebelsky, G., *op. cit.*, p. 78
49. Zagrebelsky, G., *op. cit.*, p. 59
50. Jossa, G., *op. cit.*, p. 119

Bibliography

Bammel, E. and Moule, C.F.D., *Jesus and the Politics of His Day*. 1984

Bammel, E. (ed.), *The Trial of Jesus*. 1970

Blinzler, J., *The Trial of Jesus*. 1959

Brandon, S.G.F., *Jesus and the Zealots*. 1967

Brandon, S.G.F., *The Trial of Jesus of Nazareth*. 1968

Braybrooke, M., *Time to Meet*. 1990

Braybrooke, M., *Christian-Jewish Dialogue*. 2000

Braybrooke, M., *Commentaries on the Gospels and Life of Jesus*

Brown, R.E., *The Death of the Messiah* (2 vols.). 1993, 1994

Catchpole, D., *The Trial of Jesus*. 1971

Chandler, W.M., *The Trial of Jesus from a Lawyer's Standpoint* (2 vols.). 2013

Crossan, J.D., *Who Killed Jesus?* 1995

Cullman, O., *Jesus and the Revolutionaries of His Time*. 1970

Grieve, V., *The Trial of Jesus*. 1990

Hengel, M., *Was Jesus a Revolutionist?* 1971

Hengel, M., *Crucifixion*. 1977

Horsley, R.A., *'The Death of Jesus'* in *Studying the Historical Jesus*. 1994

Kelber, W.H. (ed.), *The Passion in Mark*. 1976

Kilpatrick, G.D., *The Trial of Jesus*. 1953

Last, H., *'Coercitio'*, 1957

Lawrence, J.W., *The Six Trials of Jesus*. 1927, 1977

Légasse, S., *The Trial of Jesus*. 1997

Limbaugh, D., *Jesus on Trial*. 2014

Lohse, E., *The History of the Death and Suffering of Jesus Christ*. 1967

Mack, B., *A Myth of Innocence*. 1988

Moule, C.F.D., *Jesus and the Politics of His Day*. 1984

Richards, K., *Jesus on Trial*. 2001

Rivkin, E., *What Crucified Jesus?: Messianism, Pharisaism, and the Development of Christianity*. 1997

Robinson, M., *Jesus Christ's Trial, Death and Resurrection*. 2014

Ryken, P.E. and Boice, J.M., *Jesus on Trial*. 2002

Sherwin-White, A.N., *Roman Society and Roman Law in the New Testament*. 1963

Sloyan, G.S., *Jesus on Trial*. 2006

Stalker, J., *The Trial and Death of Jesus Christ*. 1894, 2011

Theissen, G. and Merz, A., *'Jesus as Martyr: The Passion of Jesus'* in *The Historical Jesus*. 1964

Watson, A., *The Trial of Jesus*. 2012

Winter, P., *On the Trial of Jesus*. 1961, 1974

Winters, J., *The Trial of Jesus*. 1961

Index